Dr. Seuss

Jill Foran

www.av2books.com

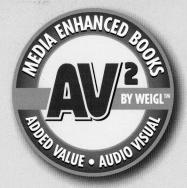

RAP 843 4625

AV² provides enriched content that supplements and complements this boo[k]
Weigl's AV² books strive to create inspired learning and engage young mind[s]
in a total learning experience.

Your AV² Media Enhanced books come alive with...

Audio
Listen to sections of
the book read aloud.

Key Words
Study vocabulary, and
complete a matching
word activity.

Go to **www.av2books.com**,
and enter this book's
unique code.

Video
Watch informative
video clips.

Quizzes
Test your knowledge.

BOOK CODE

M 5 9 2 1 2 6

Embedded Weblinks
Gain additional information
for research.

Slide Show
View images and
captions, and prepare
a presentation.

AV² by Weigl brings you media
enhanced books that support
active learning.

Try This!
Complete activities and
hands-on experiments.

... and much, much more

Published by AV² by Weigl
350 5th Avenue, 59th Floor
New York, NY 10118

Website: www.weigl.com www.av2books.com
Copyright ©2013 AV² by Weigl

Library of Congress Cataloging-in-Publication Data

Foran, Jill.
 Dr. Seuss / Jill Foran.
     p. cm. -- (Remarkable writers)
 Includes index.
 ISBN 978-1-61913-059-3 (hard cover : alk. paper) -- ISBN 978-1-61913-595-6 (soft cover : alk. paper) -- ISBN 978-1-61913-717-2 (ebook)
 1. Seuss, Dr.--Juvenile literature. 2. Authors, American--20th century--Biography--Juvenile literature. 3. Illustrators--United States--Biography--Juvenile literature. 4. Children's
literature--Authorship--Juvenile literature. I. Title.
 PS3513.E2Z67 2013
 813'.52--dc23
 [B]
                                      2012003163

Printed in the United States of America, in North Mankato, Minnesota
3 4 5 6 7 8 9 0 18 17 16 15 14

062014
WEP040614

Senior Editor: Heather Kissock
Design: Terry Paulhus

Weigl acknowledges Getty Images as its primary photo supplier for this title.
Random House Children's Books, a division of Random House, Inc.: pages 5, 12, 18, 19, 20, 21 (©Dr. Seuss Enterprises, L.P. 1937, renewed 1965).

Contents

AV² Book Code 2

Introducing Dr. Seuss 4

Early Life 6

Growing Up 8

Developing Skills 10

Timeline of Dr. Seuss 12

Early Achievements 14

Tricks of the Trade 16

Remarkable Books 18

From Big Ideas to Books 22

Dr. Seuss Today 24

Fan Information 26

Write a Biography 28

Test Yourself 29

Writing Terms 30

Key Words / Index 31

Log on to www.av2books.com 32

Introducing Dr. Seuss

Few children's writers are as well-known and admired as Dr. Seuss. For more than 50 years, he wrote and illustrated wonderful children's books. Today, these books are still read and enjoyed by people of all ages. Dr. Seuss's imaginative stories are brought to life with his brightly colored illustrations.

People around the world recognize Dr. Seuss's characters. The Cat in the Hat, the Grinch, and Horton the elephant are just a few of the characters found in his popular children's books. Dr. Seuss's books are written in a **rhythmic**, rhyming **verse** that makes readers laugh out loud in delight. He has shown children and adults around the world that reading is great fun. Many people can recognize his writing when they hear it, even if they have not read the book it comes from.

Dr. Seuss started writing children's books when he was 30 years old. It was the beginning of a long and successful career.

Dr. Seuss claimed that the reason he wrote so well for children was because he never grew up himself. He often said that everything he wrote or illustrated was created for his own amusement. His work continues to amuse millions of readers all over the world.

👉 Dr. Seuss was known for creating strange yet funny characters.

Writers are often inspired to record the stories of people who lead interesting lives. The story of another person's life is called a biography. A biography can tell the story of any person, from authors such as Dr. Seuss, to inventors, presidents, and sports stars.

When writing a biography, authors must first collect information about their subject. This information may come from a book about the person's life, a news article about one of his or her accomplishments, or a review of his or her work. Libraries and the internet will have much of this information. Most biographers will also interview their subjects. Personal accounts provide a great deal of information and a unique point of view. When some basic details about the person's life have been collected, it is time to begin writing a biography.

As you read about Dr. Seuss, you will be introduced to the important parts of a biography. Use these tips and the examples provided to learn how to write about an author or any other remarkable person.

Early Life

Dr. Seuss was born Theodor Seuss Geisel on March 2, 1904. He was named after his father, Theodor Robert. From the time Dr. Seuss was young, his family and friends called him Ted. Ted grew up in the town of Springfield, Massachusetts. His father was a kind man who worked in a **brewery** for many years. Ted's mother, Henrietta, worked in a bakery. She also took care of Ted, his older sister, Marnie, and his younger sister, Henrietta. Both parents were of German **descent**, and their children grew up speaking German and English.

"Children want the same things adults want. To laugh, to be challenged, to be entertained and delighted."
—Dr. Seuss

The Geisels were a close family, and they had many happy times together. They also experienced some hardships. When Ted was 3 years old, his youngest sister, Henrietta, died of **pneumonia**. The entire family mourned the loss.

When Ted was a little boy, he would fall asleep every night listening to his mother recite poems. She made them up for customers while working in the bakery each day. They were rhymes about different pie flavors. The poems had a fast, catchy rhythm that Ted really liked.

📖 Springfield has built a sculpture garden devoted to Dr. Seuss and his characters, including the Cat in the Hat.

Theodor and Henrietta encouraged their children to read. They would often bring Ted and Marnie to the local library. Ted would check out as many books as he could carry. He loved to read, and before he was even 10 years old, he was reading books that were written for adults.

Along with reading, Ted also loved to draw. He would spend hours at the Springfield Zoo, watching the different animals. Then he would go home and draw the animals he had seen. But Ted's animals never looked much like those at the zoo. He was not content to just copy them. He had to make them look original. Ted's animals were **bizarre** copies of the real ones, and he gave them equally bizarre names. Henrietta was very proud of her son's artwork, and she encouraged him to keep drawing. She even let him draw on the attic walls.

Ted Geisel worked on illustrations at his home. Although he was famous as an illustrator, he never had formal art classes.

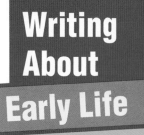

Writing About Early Life

A person's early years have a strong influence on his or her future. Parents, teachers, and friends can have a large impact on how a person thinks, feels, and behaves. These effects are strong enough to last throughout childhood, and often a person's lifetime.

In order to write about a person's early life, biographers must find answers to the following questions.

1 Where and when was the person born?

2 What is known about the person's family and friends?

3 Did the person grow up in unusual circumstances?

Growing Up

Ted was well liked by his peers when he was growing up, but there was a difficult period during his youth when he was bullied at school. In 1914, World War I began, and the United States declared war against Germany in 1917. In the United States, people of German descent were judged harshly. Some people in Springfield insulted the Geisels because the family had a German background. During this period, Ted was unfairly mocked at school. This confused him and often made him feel very lonely.

"Humor ... is more than just a matter of laughing. If you can see things out of whack, then you can see how things can be in whack."
—*Ted Geisel*

Ted worked hard to rise above the taunts of his schoolmates. He was shy, but he was also very funny. In 1917, he entered Springfield's Central High School. Ted began to write and draw for the school newspaper. He also acted in a few school plays. It did not take long for Ted to become known for his humor and creativity.

Get to Know Massachusetts

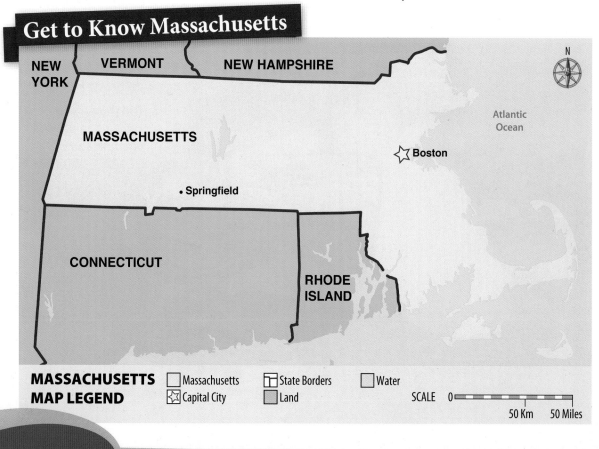

NEW YORK

VERMONT

NEW HAMPSHIRE

MASSACHUSETTS

Atlantic Ocean

☆ Boston

• Springfield

CONNECTICUT

RHODE ISLAND

MASSACHUSETTS MAP LEGEND
☐ Massachusetts   ⊞ State Borders   ☐ Water
✩ Capital City   ☐ Land   SCALE   0 ▭▭▭▭ 50 Km   50 Miles

Ted's years at Springfield's Central High School were busy ones. Although his father wanted him to join the school's sports teams, Ted was much more interested in working for the newspaper. It was called the *Central Recorder*. He often wrote funny one-line **quips** known as "grinds." He also contributed poems, **satires,** and cartoons to the *Central Recorder*. The school paper included so much of Ted's work that he often had to use a **pseudonym.** His pseudonym was T. S. LeSieg. The last name was Geisel spelled backward.

Ted received good grades throughout high school. One of his favorite subjects was English. This was partly because he had an English teacher who inspired him. The teacher's name was Edwin A. "Red" Smith. Ted once said that it was Red Smith who **motivated** him to write. Before long, it was time for Ted to decide where he should go to college. He chose to go to Dartmouth College in Hanover, New Hampshire, because that was where Red had gone.

After he became famous, Ted Geisel donated generously to Dartmouth College. The medical school of Dartmouth is now named the Geisel School of Medicine.

Writing About Growing Up

Some people know what they want to achieve in life from a very young age. Others do not decide until much later. In any case, it is important for biographers to discuss when and how their subjects make these decisions. Using the information they collect, biographers try to answer the following questions about their subjects' paths in life.

1 Who had the most influence on the person?

2 Did he or she receive assistance from others?

3 Did the person have a positive attitude?

Developing Skills

Ted began classes at Dartmouth College in the fall of 1921. He **majored** in English, but his true interest in college was Dartmouth's humor magazine, the *Jack-O-Lantern*. Ted discovered the magazine soon after he arrived at Dartmouth. Almost immediately, he began contributing cartoons. He made many good friends at the magazine. The college students admired his work and thought he was funny. By the end of his junior year, Ted was elected editor of the *Jack-O-Lantern*. He had worked toward this position since he arrived at Dartmouth College.

"You can get help from teachers, but you are going to have to learn a lot by yourself, sitting alone in a room."
—*Ted Geisel*

Ted was a good editor, but he did not keep the position for very long. During his last year at Dartmouth, he and some friends were caught breaking a school rule. As punishment, Ted lost the position of editor. Of course, this did not stop him from working

for the magazine. He still contributed many articles, only now he used pseudonyms instead of his real name. It was at that time that Ted first began using the name "Seuss," which was his mother's maiden name. It was also during this time that Ted recognized the power of joining words and pictures.

🖋 As the editor of the *Jack-O-Lantern*, Ted was responsible for the content of the magazine. This included both articles and pictures.

While at Dartmouth, Ted was so busy with the *Jack-O-Lantern* that he had little time left over for his regular classes. There was only one class that really held his interest. It was a creative writing course taught by a man named Ben Pressey. Ben was very supportive of Ted's writing. He inspired Ted in college the same way that Red Smith had in high school.

After Ted graduated from Dartmouth, he still had no idea what he wanted to do for a living. In the fall of 1925, he moved to England to attend Oxford University. While there, he met and fell in love with a fellow student named Helen Palmer. Although he and Helen were very happy together, Ted could not find happiness in his studies. He spent more time doodling in his notebook than he did listening to his professors. Helen admired Ted's doodles and drawings. She helped convince Ted that he should try illustrating for a living. Ted left Oxford to pursue new goals.

Oxford University in England is one of the world's oldest and best-known universities.

Writing About Developing Skills

Every remarkable person has skills and traits that make him or her noteworthy. Some people have natural talent, while others practice diligently. For most, it is a combination of the two. One of the most important things that a biographer can do is to tell the story of how the subject developed his or her talents.

1 What was the person's education?

2 What was the person's first job or work experience?

3 What obstacles did the person overcome?

Timeline of Dr. Seuss

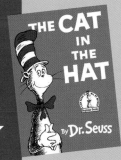

1957

The Cat in the Hat, Ted's best-known book, is published. It becomes a best-seller for decades after. In 2009, 52 years after it was originally published, it sold more than 450,000 copies.

1904

Theodor Seuss Geisel is born in Springfield, Massachusetts, on March 2. His parents, Theodor and Henrietta, had moved to the United States from Germany.

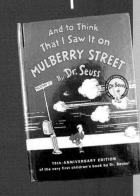

1937

Ted publishes his first book, *And to Think That I Saw It on Mulberry Street*. Twenty-seven publishers reject it before it is finally printed. The steady rhythm of the rhymes was inspired by the sound of a ship's engine.

1927

Ted begins submitting his writing and drawings to magazines such as *Life* and *Vanity Fair*. Eventually, *The Saturday Evening Post* purchases a cartoon—the first ever published under the name Dr. Seuss. This same year, Ted marries Helen Palmer.

1921

Ted attends Dartmouth College and becomes editor-in-chief of its humor magazine, the *Jack-O-Lantern*. After four years, he graduates with a degree in English.

1991

Ted dies on September 24 at the age of 87. By this time, Ted has earned two Academy Awards, two Emmy Awards, and a Peabody Award, in addition to a Pulitzer Prize. In 2008, he is added to the California Hall of Fame.

1998

The National Education Association creates Read Across America, a day dedicated to inspiring young readers. The NEA chooses Ted's birthday, March 2, for this event to honor his life's work.

WEDNESDAY, MARCH 2ⁿᵈ IS . . .

National Read Across america day

1960

Ted's publisher had bet that Ted could not write a best-selling book using 50 different words. In 1960, Ted writes *Green Eggs and Ham* using only 50 words. He wins $50 on the bet. His wife, Helen Palmer Geisel, also wrote children's books around this time.

1984

Ted wins the Pulitzer Prize. The award is given "for his special contribution over nearly half a century to the education and enjoyment of America's children and their parents."

1966

Ted's book *How the Grinch Stole Christmas!* becomes an animated television special. The special became widely popular and is still broadcast during the Christmas season to this day.

Early Achievements

After leaving Oxford University, Ted spent some time traveling around Europe. He toured parts of Austria, Italy, and France, and lived for a short time in Paris. In February 1927, he returned to the United States and moved back into his parents' house in Springfield. At the time, Ted did not have a job. However, he had a clear goal. He wanted to get his cartoons published.

> "I like nonsense. It wakes up the brain cells. Fantasy is a necessary ingredient in living."
> —Dr. Seuss

Every day, Ted sat at his father's desk and drew. He sent his drawings out to popular magazines. After many rejections, a magazine called *The Saturday Evening Post* bought one of his cartoons for $25. Soon after that success, Ted moved to New York. He showed his drawings to the editor of a magazine called *Judge* and was quickly hired as a writer and artist. In November 1927, Ted married his sweetheart from college, Helen Palmer.

Ted worked very hard at *Judge*. He drew funny cartoons, and wrote short, humorous essays. Most of these contributions were given the **byline** "Seuss." It was also during his time at *Judge* that Ted added the title "Dr." to his name. He claimed that the name "Dr. Seuss" made him seem more **credible.**

📖 *The Saturday Evening Post* was one of the best-known magazines in America when Dr. Seuss was first published in it.

Ted's work at *Judge* led to one of the luckiest breaks of his life. He drew a cartoon that featured a knight in bed with a dragon nuzzling him. The **caption** beneath the cartoon read, "Darn it all, another dragon. And just after I'd sprayed the whole castle with Flit." Flit was an **insecticide** that people used to kill insects. When the owners of Flit saw the cartoon, they were impressed. The cartoon led to a contract for Ted to write all of Flit's advertisements. These ads became famous.

Despite his success in advertising, Ted wanted to work on other projects. He was hired to illustrate a book called *Boners,* which was published in 1931. The book was very popular, and Ted's drawings received great reviews. However, Ted did not receive any **royalties** from the sales. As an artist, he had been paid a **flat fee** for his work. Ted decided that if he wanted to make a living, he would have to write as well as draw.

Writing About Early Achievements

No two people take the same path to success. Some people work very hard for a long time before achieving their goals. Others may take advantage of a fortunate turn of events. Biographers must make special note of the traits and qualities that allow their subjects to succeed.

1 What was the person's most important early success?

2 What process does the person use in his or her work?

3 Which of the person's traits was most helpful in his or her work?

Judge Magazine was a weekly magazine that was published in the United States from 1881 to 1947.

Tricks of the Trade

Writing a story or a poem can be challenging, but it can also be very rewarding. Some writers have trouble coming up with ideas, while others have so many ideas that they do not know where to start. Dr. Seuss had special writing habits that young writers can follow to develop their ideas into great stories.

Keep Your Eyes and Ears Open

Many writers get ideas by watching people and listening to conversations. If you pay attention, you will see that most people say and do all sorts of interesting things. These things can inspire writers to develop characters or to write funny scenes. Dr. Seuss found a great deal of inspiration in conversations or things he overheard. He would use his own imagination to make them more amusing.

Write, Write, Write

Sometimes, the easiest way to finish a poem or a story is to write as much as possible in a first **draft.** This way, a writer can get all of his or her ideas down on paper. Then, the writer can decide which parts to keep. Very few writers have ever produced a great story in just one draft. Instead, they may review their first draft to see which parts should stay and what needs to be **revised.** Dr. Seuss claimed that the secret to his success was writing too much. He would often write and draw more than 500 pages of material for a 60-page book.

The Creative Process

Most writers have different opinions about when is the best time to write. Some work best late at night when everyone else is asleep. Others claim that they are most productive early in the morning. There are also differing approaches to the writing process. Some writers need to make a detailed outline. This is a good idea for new writers, as it will help them to organize their thoughts. Some writers do not use an outline; they simply begin writing and let their ideas flow. Dr. Seuss had no set pattern to his creative process. Sometimes, he would write and illustrate a book all at once. Other times, he would write a story and add the illustrations later.

> "I know my stuff all looks like it was rattled off in twenty-three seconds, but every word is a struggle."
> —*Ted Geisel*

It Takes Dedication

Writing takes dedication and discipline. Dr. Seuss spent at least eight hours per day working on his stories and illustrations. It was this dedication, along with his ability to make work fun, that led to so many successful books.

Dr. Seuss often wrote or drew several different versions of his books. He would revise his work until it was right.

Remarkable Books

D r. Seuss had a long and successful writing career. Although most of his books were written for children, adults love his stories, too. Today, many parents who read Dr. Seuss books with their children can remember reading the same books when they were young.

And to Think That I Saw It on Mulberry Street

Dr. Seuss's first book tells the story of Marco, a young boy with a wonderful imagination. Every day, Marco's father asks him what he has seen on the way to and from school. Marco tells his father imaginative stories, but his father gets impatient and tells Marco not to tell tales. One afternoon, while Marco is walking along Mulberry Street, he sees a horse and a wagon. These are not exciting sights to young Marco, so he imagines different sights instead. Before long, a wonderful, imaginary parade is marching down Mulberry Street. When Marco returns home, his father asks him what he has seen. What Marco decides to tell his father will amuse and surprise readers.

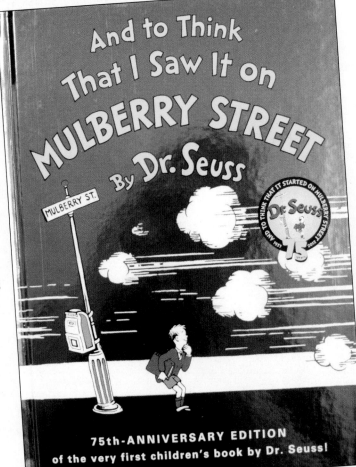

Horton Hatches the Egg

Horton Hatches the Egg is a touching story about the rewards of keeping a promise. The story begins when a lazy bird named Mayzie becomes tired of sitting on her egg. She spots a kind elephant named Horton and begs him to sit on her nest while she is away on vacation. Horton agrees to sit up in the tree on Mayzie's nest. He sits and sits, but Mayzie does not return. Horton endures many challenges while sitting in the tree. Still, he never leaves the nest because of his promise to Mayzie. When the egg finally hatches, no one is more surprised than Horton at what pops out.

McElligot's Pool

This book is about imagination, patience, and hope. The main character of the tale is Marco, who was also the hero in *And to Think That I Saw It on Mulberry Street*. This time, Marco is trying to fish at McElligot's Pool, but he is told that he will not catch anything because the pool is full of junk. Marco imagines that McElligot's Pool winds its way under farms and villages and connects to the sea. He pictures different kinds of fascinating fish swimming in the pool.

AWARDS
McElligot's Pool
1947 Caldecott
Honor Award
1950 Young Reader's
Choice Award

How the Grinch Stole Christmas!

This story is enjoyed by many children during the Christmas season. A grumpy creature named the Grinch lives on top of Mount Crumpet, high above the town of Whoville. The Grinch dislikes just about everything, but he especially dislikes Christmas. He cannot stand the presents, feasting, singing, and noise. He has put up with Christmas for too many years. This year, he decides to put an end to all the Christmas cheer in Whoville. On Christmas Eve, the Grinch steals every present, treat, and decoration in town. He is certain that everyone in Whoville will be devastated. However, when Christmas Day arrives, the Grinch is greeted by a surprise that changes him for the better.

The Cat in the Hat

When two children find themselves at home alone on a rainy day, the Cat in the Hat comes to play. The children are bored because they cannot go outside. Suddenly, a cat in a tall hat comes through the front door, bringing all kinds of excitement. The children watch, amazed, as the Cat in the Hat and his friends make a terrible mess of the house. How will they clean up the mess before their mother comes home?

Green Eggs and Ham

The funny book *Green Eggs and Ham* was written for early readers. The story follows a pesky character named Sam-I-Am. He is trying to get another character in the book to eat green eggs and ham. Although the other character says that he cannot stand the meal, Sam-I-Am keeps bothering him until he finally agrees to taste it. What happens next will be a great surprise to readers.

The Lorax

This book is about the dangers of greed and **environmental** destruction. The story begins when a beast called a Once-ler discovers a beautiful forest. The forest is filled with happy animals, fresh water, and countless Truffula trees. These beautiful trees have tufts that are softer than silk. The Once-ler decides to use the tufts to knit something called a Thneed. He knows he can sell the Thneed and become rich. When the Once-ler chops down a Truffula tree, a short, brown creature pops out of the stump. The creature is called the Lorax, and he speaks for the trees. The Lorax asks the Once-ler not to cut down any more Truffulas, but the Once-ler ignores his pleas. Soon, the entire forest is in danger.

From Big Ideas to Books

The first book that Ted wrote and illustrated was a children's alphabet book. It was filled with his colorful, imaginative drawings. He sent his new **manuscript** to several publishers in the United States, but not one of these companies was interested in publishing it. After these rejections, Ted decided to forget about his children's book. He went back to his work in advertising.

"Simple, short sentences don't always work. You have to do tricks with pacing, alternate long sentences with short, to keep it vital and alive.... Virtually every page is a cliffhanger—you've got to force them to turn it."
—*Ted Geisel*

Ted did not attempt to write a book again until 1936. That year, he toured Europe with Helen. They returned home on a ship, sailing from France to New York. During the journey, Ted could not stop listening to the rhythm of the ship's engines. After a while, he began making up silly words and rhymes to go along with the whirring sound. He soon found himself chanting the words, "And that is a story that no one can beat; and to think that I saw it on Mulberry Street." Ted decided that he needed to write and illustrate a story to go along with these words.

The Publishing Process

Publishing companies receive hundreds of manuscripts from authors each year. Only a few manuscripts become books. Publishers must be sure that a manuscript will sell many copies. As a result, publishers reject most of the manuscripts they receive. Once a manuscript has been accepted, it goes through

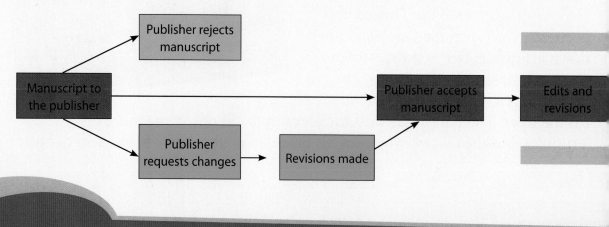

It took Ted six months to write and illustrate the book. When he was finished, he presented it to about 30 different publishers. It was rejected by all of them. They told Ted that the book would not sell because it was too different.

After yet another unsuccessful meeting with a publisher, Ted became very discouraged. He decided to take his book home and burn it. As he trudged back to his apartment, Ted bumped into an old friend from Dartmouth College named Mike McClintock. Ted told him about the book. Mike, an editor for Vanguard Press, asked him if he could read the book. Within one hour, Ted had signed a contract to have his first book published.

The book was titled *And to Think That I Saw It on Mulberry Street.* Published under the name Dr. Seuss in 1937, it quickly became a bestseller. Over the next three years, Dr. Seuss produced three more children's books: *The 500 Hats of Bartholomew Cubbins, The King's Stilts,* and *Horton Hatches the Egg.*

🖐 Mulberry Street is the name of a street in Springfield, Massachusetts, 1 mile (1.6 km) southwest of Dr. Seuss's boyhood home.

many stages before it is published. Often, authors change their work to follow an editor's suggestions. Once the book is published, some authors receive royalties. This is money based on book sales.

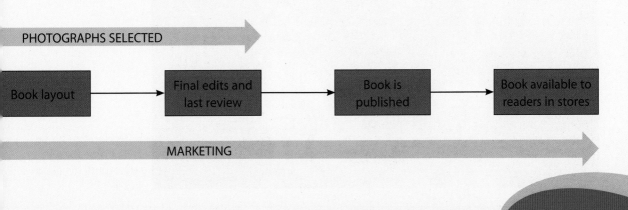

PHOTOGRAPHS SELECTED

Book layout → Final edits and last review → Book is published → Book available to readers in stores

MARKETING

Dr. Seuss Today

Ted and Helen Geisel moved to La Jolla, California, in 1948. Ted lived and worked there for the rest of his life. The Seuss's property in La Jolla was the highest point in the area. It was also the location of an abandoned observation tower, which stood overlooking the Pacific Ocean. Ted and Helen built a pink stucco house around the tower, and Ted converted the tower room into an office.

Although Ted never had children of his own, he connected with children around the globe through his books. Sadly, in 1967, Helen Geisel passed away. Shortly after, Ted married Audrey Diamond, a longtime friend.

In 1984, Dr. Seuss was awarded a Pulitzer Prize for his special contribution to children's literature. He was honored for his work, which spanned 50 years.

As he grew older, Dr. Seuss continued to produce bestsellers despite his failing health. He did not want to retire. Ted was not ready to give up the joys of writing and illustrating. In 1990, Dr. Seuss came out with a book called *Oh, the Places You'll Go*. The book was on the *New York Times* bestseller list longer than any other children's book. Unfortunately, it was Ted's last book.

⋓ Ted lived in his La Jolla home for 43 years, until his death in 1991.

On September 24, 1991, Ted passed away in his sleep. His death was mourned by devoted fans, young and old, around the world. Along with his books, Ted's **legacy** includes a charitable fund called the Dr. Seuss Foundation. Today, the foundation continues to contribute money and resources to libraries, charities, and zoos.

Ted Geisel dedicated much of his career to making reading fun. He made a major contribution to reading and children's **literature.** Today, schools across the United States hold Read Across America day each year on his birthday. On this day, students, teachers, and other members of the community share books and enjoy reading circles.

✐ Dr. Seuss's Cat in the Hat is the mascot of Read Across America day. Both children and adults alike often wear Cat in the Hat hats as part of the event.

Writing About the Person Today

The biography of any living person is an ongoing story. People have new ideas, start new projects, and deal with challenges. For their work to be meaningful, biographers must include up-to-date information about their subjects. Through research, biographers try to answer the following questions.

1 Has the person received awards or recognition for accomplishments?

2 What is the person's life's work?

3 How have the person's accomplishments served others?

Fan Information

Dr. Seuss has written wonderful books that make reading fun. He has millions of dedicated fans. Throughout his career, Ted received great quantities of fan mail. As early as 1957, he was receiving more than 9,000 pounds (4,082 kilograms) of fan mail each year. Ted was sent letters of gratitude, valentines, drawings, and countless birthday cards. After he published *Green Eggs and Ham* in 1960, Ted began receiving strange packages. People began sending him green eggs and ham!

Dr. Seuss's creations have appeared in his books, as well as movies and television specials based on the books. His characters now also appear on the Seussville.com website.

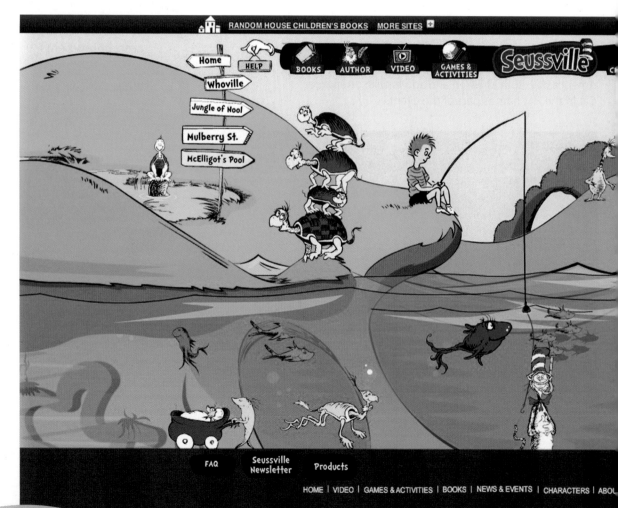

Ted was always busy. He usually did not have the time to respond to most of his mail. Still, Ted did attend many book signings. Once in a while, he made appearances at schools and special events. He was also known for welcoming curious fans into his home in La Jolla.

Today, more than 600 million copies of Dr. Seuss's books have been sold. They have been translated into more than 20 different languages and have been turned into television specials and feature films.

Many fans have created impressive websites to share information about Dr. Seuss. To find websites on Dr. Seuss and his inspiring life and work, type "Dr. Seuss" or "Theodor Seuss Geisel" into a search engine such as Google or Bing.

Write a Biography

All of the parts of a biography work together to tell the story of a person's life. Find out how these elements combine by writing a biography. Begin by choosing a person whose story fascinates you. You will have to research the person's life by using library books and reliable websites. You can also e-mail the person or write him or her a letter. The person might agree to answer your questions directly.

Use a concept web, such as the one below, to guide you in writing the biography. Answer each of the questions listed using the information you have gathered. Each heading on the concept web will form an important part of the person's story.

Parts of a Biography

Early Life

Where and when was the person born?

What is known about the person's family and friends?

Did the person grow up in unusual circumstances?

Growing Up

Who had the most influence on the person?

Did he or she receive assistance from others?

Did the person have a positive attitude?

Developing Skills

What was the person's education?

What was the person's first job or work experience?

What obstacles did the person overcome?

Person Today

Has the person received awards or recognition for accomplishments?

What is the person's life's work?

How have the person's accomplishments served others?

Early Achievements

What was the person's most important early success?

What processes does this person use in his or her work?

Which of the person's traits were most helpful in his or her work?

Test Yourself

1 When and where was Theodor Seuss Geisel born?

2 Ted's mother recited poems to him when he was a little boy. What were they about?

3 What was the name of the newspaper that Ted wrote for in high school?

4 What was Ted's pseudonym for the *Central Recorder*?

5 With whom did Ted meet and fall in love while he was in England?

6 Where did Dr. Seuss live and work for most of his adult life?

7 What college did Ted attend in the United States?

8 For what product was Ted contracted to write and illustrate advertisements?

9 What was Ted's first published children's book?

10 How many Dr. Seuss books have been sold over the years?

ANSWERS
1. Dr. Seuss was born on March 2, 1904, in Springfield, Massachusetts. 2. The poems were about different flavors of pies. 3. Ted wrote for the *Central Recorder*. 4. Ted's pseudonym was T. S. LeSieg, "Geisel" spelled backward. 5. Helen Palmer. 6. La Jolla, California 7. Dartmouth College 8. Flit Insecticide 9. *And to Think That I Saw It on Mulberry Street* 10. More than 600 million books have been sold

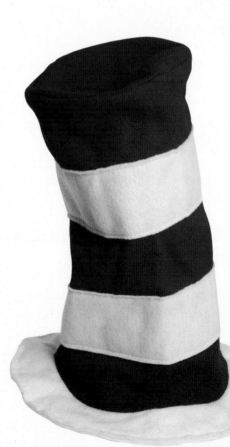

Writing Terms

The field of writing has its own language. Understanding some of the more common writing terms will allow you to discuss your ideas about books.

action: the moving events of a work of fiction

antagonist: the person in the story who opposes the main character

autobiography: a history of a person's life written by that person

biography: a written account of another person's life

character: a person in a story, poem, or play

climax: the most exciting moment or turning point in a story

episode: a scene or short piece of action in a story

fiction: stories about characters and events that are not real

foreshadow: hinting at something that is going to happen later in the book

imagery: a written description of a thing or idea that brings an image to mind

narrator: the speaker of the story who relates the events

nonfiction: writing that deals with real people and events

novel: published writing of considerable length that portrays characters within a story

plot: the order of events in a work of fiction

protagonist: the leading character of a story; often a likable character

resolution: the end of the story, when the conflict is settled

scene: a single episode in a story

setting: the place and time in which a work of fiction occurs

theme: an idea that runs throughout a work of fiction

Key Words

bizarre: odd or unusual

brewery: a place where beer is made

byline: a printed line beneath the title of a piece of writing that gives the author's name

caption: a short piece of writing that describes or explains an illustration

credible: trustworthy or reliable

descent: family background

draft: a rough copy of a story

environmental: relating to the natural world

flat fee: a fixed amount of money paid for a story

insecticide: a substance used for killing insects

legacy: something handed down to future generations

literature: writing of lasting value, including plays, poems, and novels

major: a student's main subject of study

manuscript: a draft of a story before it is published

motivated: encouraged someone to do something

pneumonia: an illness characterized by an inflammation of the lungs

pseudonym: a fictitious name used by an author; a pen name

quips: short, clever remarks

revised: changed

rhythmic: having a patterned beat or rhythm

royalties: payments made to an author based on sales of his or her work

satires: stories that make fun of human weaknesses

verse: writing arranged with a rhythm and usually a rhyme

Index

And to Think That I Saw It on Mulberry Street 12, 18, 19, 23, 29

Cat in the Hat, The 12, 20

Dartmouth College 9
Diamond, Audrey 24

Flit Insecticide 15, 29

Green Eggs and Ham 13, 21, 26

Horton Hatches the Egg 19, 23
How the Grinch Stole Christmas! 13, 20

Jack-O-Lantern 10, 11, 12
Judge 14, 15

La Jolla, California 24, 27, 29
LeSieg, T. S. 9, 29
Lorax, The 21

McClintock, Mike 23
McElligot's Pool 18, 19

Oh, The Places You'll Go 24
Oxford University 11, 14

Palmer, Helen 11, 13, 12, 14, 29

Saturday Evening Post, The 12, 14
Smith, Edwin A. "Red" 9, 11
Springfield, Massachusetts 6, 8, 12, 14, 23, 29

Log on to www.av2books.com

AV² by Weigl brings you media enhanced books that support active learning. Go to www.av2books.com, and enter the special code found on page 2 of this book. You will gain access to enriched and enhanced content that supplements and complements this book. Content includes video, audio, weblinks, quizzes, a slide show, and activities.

Audio
Listen to sections of the book read aloud.

Video
Watch informative video clips.

Embedded Weblinks
Gain additional information for research.

Try This!
Complete activities and hands-on experiments.

WHAT'S ONLINE?

Try This!	Embedded Weblinks	Video	EXTRA FEATURES
Complete an activity about your childhood.	Learn more about Dr. Seuss's life.	Watch a video about Dr. Seuss	**Audio** Listen to sections of the book read aloud.
Try this timeline activity.	Learn more about Dr. Seuss's achievements.	Watch this interview with Dr. Seuss.	**Key Words** Study vocabulary, and complete a matching word activity.
See what you know about the publishing process.	Check out this site about Dr. Seuss.		**Slide Show** View images and captions and prepare a presentation
Test your knowledge of writing terms.			**Quizzes** Test your knowledge.
Write a biography.			

AV² was built to bridge the gap between print and digital. We encourage you to tell us what you like and what you want to see in the future.

Sign up to be an AV² Ambassador at www.av2books.com/ambassador.